Working With Words

A HANDBOOK FOR MEDIA WRITERS AND EDITORS

Fourth Edition
Exercise Book

Brian S. Brooks
Missouri School of Journalism

James L. Pinson
Eastern Michigan University

Jean Gaddy Wilson
Missouri School of Journalism and New Directions for News

Bedford/St Martin's   Boston • New York

Copyright © 2000 by Bedford/St. Martin's

All rights reserved.

Instructors who have adopted *Working With Words: A Handbook for Media Writers and Editors,* Fourth Edition, as a textbook for a course are authorized to duplicate portions of this manual for their students.

Manufactured in the United States of America.

5 4 3 2 1
f e d c b

For information, write: Bedford/St. Martin's, 75 Arlington Street, Boston, MA 02116   (617-399-4000)

ISBN: 0-312-20982-7

Preface

From years spent working as copy editors and journalism teachers, we've seen the kinds of mistakes most often made by students and professionals. We've drawn on that experience to put together these examples of the most common pitfalls.

We designed this workbook to give a thorough and systematic drill in the language skills required to become — and to excel as — a reporter or editor in any of the media.

The exercises — like "Working With Words," the textbook they accompany — cover grammar, usage, wordiness, spelling, wire-service style and editing symbols. They also cover objectivity and sensitivity to unconscious sexism and racism, topics we think deserve special attention.

We've organized the exercises to follow closely the presentation in the text. When considering a new topic, we've often first provided general questions to help students develop a summary of the main points in the book. We've then provided practical exercises focusing on specific difficulties.

Students should be warned not to try to do these exercises "by ear." Those who don't read the relevant information in the text will probably score poorly. That's because we've chosen primarily to focus on those points that typically trouble students the most—the places where the rules of written English differ from how many of us actually speak.

Deprived of the ability to get many of these right by ear alone, students may find these exercises difficult at times. But we follow here the lead of good music teachers, who tell their students they'll make progress faster by practicing the harder parts more than the easier ones.

Brian S. Brooks
James L. Pinson
Jean Gaddy Wilson

Contents

Basic Skills Pretest   1

Copy-Editing Symbols   7

CHAPTER 1   Grammar Basics   9

CHAPTER 2   Phrases, Clauses and Sentences   11
　Restrictive vs. Nonrestrictive   13
　Sentence Errors   15

CHAPTER 3   Subjects and Objects: Nouns and Pronouns   17
　Common Nouns vs. Proper Nouns   19
　The Forms Nouns Take   21
　Pronoun Forms and Agreement   25
　Problems With Pronoun Case   27
　Who vs. Whom, Whoever vs. Whomever; CHAPTER 2: That vs. Which   29

CHAPTER 4   Subject-Verb Agreement   31
　Subject-Verb Agreement, No. 1   33
　Subject-Verb Agreement, No. 2   35

CHAPTER 5   Verbs   37
　Tenses, No. 1   39
　Tenses, No. 2   43
　Voice   45
　Mood   47
　Nouns Used as Verbs   49

CHAPTER 6   Modifiers   51
　Comparative Forms of Adjectives and Adverbs   53
　Adjectives vs. Adverbs   57
　Coordinate Adjectives vs. Compound Modifiers   59
　Articles   61
　Dangling Participles and Misplaced Modifiers   63

CHAPTER 7	Connecting Words 65
	Connecting Words, No. 2 67
CHAPTER 8	Usage 69
	Distinctions Made by Wire Services 69
	Substantives and Verbs 71
	Modifiers and Connectives 73
	Assorted Usage Problems 75
CHAPTER 9	Punctuation 77
	Punctuating Quotations and Paraphrases 79
CHAPTER 10	Spelling Relief 81
	One Word, Two Words or Hyphenated? A-M 83
	One Word, Two Words or Hyphenated? N-Z 85
CHAPTER 11	Writing as a Journalist 87
	Objectivity 87
CHAPTER 12	Conciseness 89
	Conciseness, No. 2 91
CHAPTER 13	Sexism, Racism and Other "isms" 93
CHAPTER 14	Writing News That's Fit for Print 97
	Wire-Service Style Summary, No. 1 101
	Wire-Service Style Summary, No. 2 107
CHAPTER 15	Writing News for Broadcast 109
CHAPTER 16	Writing News for the New Media 111
REVIEW No. 1	Identifying Parts of Speech 113
REVIEW No. 2	Identifying Verbals 115
REVIEW No. 3	Identifying Parts of a Sentence 117
REVIEW No. 4	Final Exam 119

Basic Skills Pretest

NAME: _____

CLASS: _____

DATE: _____

This test focuses on your knowledge of the requirements of correct sentence structure, subject-predicate agreement, pronoun-antecedent agreement, pronoun case, principal parts of verbs, punctuation, and a few common spelling and usage errors.

A. Label each of the following *S* for sentence, *FR* for fragment, *R* for run-on, *FU* for fused, or *CS* for comma splice.

1. _____ The assailant fled on foot, he is described as white, about six feet tall, 180 pounds and wearing a black leather jacket.

2. _____ Several people make reproductions of high-wheeled antique bicycles, but original bikes are hard to find.

3. _____ A ring of flames shot up onstage, and standing in their midst, Garth Brooks played guitar and sang.

4. _____ The Internet provider will offer accounts to individuals businesses may sign up, too.

5. _____ The taxi commission in New York is asking the city's cabdrivers — world famous for rudeness — to be polite and is teaching them, many of them foreigners who speak little English, 50 expressions, such as "Thank you for hailing me, Madam; I'd be happy to take you to Brooklyn" and "I'll do my best to avoid the potholes," but the exercise is receiving more jokes than praise.

6. _____ Even the president.

7. _____ About 67 percent of teen-age girls have sex but only because boys pressure them, according to a Seventeen magazine survey.

8. _____ The Humane Society of Springfield is sponsoring a pet walkathon Sunday, walkers need not bring a pet to participate.

9. _____ Dan Blausley pitched a no-hitter for Summerfield on Tuesday the team won 3–1 over Amantee.

10. _____ According to the St. John's County, Fla., ordinance against nude dancing, *buttocks* is defined as "the area at the rear of the human body (sometimes referred to as the gluteus maximus) which lies between two imaginary lines running parallel to the ground when a person is standing, the first or top of such lines being one-half inch below the top of the vertical cleavage of the nates (i.e., the prominence formed by the muscles running from the back of the hip to the back of the leg) and the second or bottom line being one-half inch above the lowest point of the curvature of the fleshy protuberance (sometimes referred to as the gluteal fold), and between two imaginary lines, one on each side of the body."

B. Circle the *correct* answers.

1. One of the three never (miss, misses) a deadline.
2. None of the contractors (has, have) bid on the contract.
3. Each (was, were) given a choice of seats.
4. A Sony PlayStation, along with a controller, (sell, sells) for about $100.
5. Forsyth said, "(A lot, Alot, Allot) of us don't know what he's doing."
6. The media (were, was) out in full.
7. The five-member council filed (its, their) report this morning.
8. He lectured on the evils of communism to (whoever, whomever) would listen.
9. Is this briefcase (your's, yours)?
10. But who founded the company? It was (she, her).
11. Bennington said he doubted anyone could find a happier person than (he, him).
12. (There are, There's) two to help out with farm chores now.
13. (Who's, Whose) sorry now?
14. (Us, We) citizens should have more say in it.
15. Neither of the criticisms has lost (its, it's, their) sting.
16. She said she felt (bad, badly) about missing the meeting.
17. He is the (younger, youngest) of the three brothers.
18. This is where the (Petersens', Petersen's, Petersens) live.
19. That's (she, her).
20. Between you and (I, me), nothing could be further from the truth.
21. Give the information to Steve or (me, myself).
22. The City Council will hold (its, their) next meeting Monday.
23. A reporter should check (his, his or her, their) copy.
24. (Who, Whom) did he say was the best photographer he has?
25. Most surveyed said Cola A goes down (more smoothly, smoother) than Cola B.
26. The perfume smells (sweet, sweetly).

Basic Skills Pretest (Continued)

NAME: _____
CLASS: _____
DATE: _____

27. What will the (affect, effect) be?

28. She said the plan worked (good, well).

29. He had just (laid, layed, lain, lied) down for a nap.

30. Johnson told him to (set, sit) down and rest his feet.

31. Her mother asked her to (raise, rise) up for a second.

32. She said, "I think (you're, your) sitting on my newspaper."

33. (Among, Between) the three of them, he said, they'll come up with something.

C. Circle the *correct* answers.

1. She is one of those people (who, whom) (is, are) never too busy to see a student.

2. Guess (who's, whose) coming to Pine Knob this week.

3. (Prior to, Before) the operation, she was in constant pain.

4. (While, Although) the panel (disagree, disagrees) now, at one time that wasn't the case.

5. They said they hoped to put together a proposal that (will, would) compare favorably (to, with) the one (that, which) has been submitted by Frech Corp.

6. She said she didn't know (if, whether, whether or not) she would go out for basketball next year after this losing season.

7. He was (convinced, persuaded) that he should try to (convince, persuade) others to go to the seminar.

8. Several of them plan to return to meet with (each other, one another).

9. They said they thought (she, her) to be (she, her).

10. They said they thought (she, her) was (she, her).

11. (We, Us) journalism students have it rough but not (as, so) rough as (they, them).

12. It is (she, her), not (he, him), of (who, whom) the family speaks.

13. He had just (laid, lay, layed, lain) down when the phone (rang, rung).

14. The budget (composes, comprises, is comprised of, is constituted of) six parts.

15. His vase was different (from, than) the one at the museum; compared (to, with) his, the museum's looked plain.

16. "What a (prejudice, prejudiced) thing to say!" she said.

17. Every reporter and editor did (her, his, his or her, their) part in getting out this special election edition.

18. For JoAnn and (me, myself), good night.

19. If the river (raises, rises) another foot, the road will flood.

20. The new father looked (proud, proudly) as he left the hospital with his wife and new daughter.

21. The car ran (good, well) after she gave it a tuneup.

22. Preston said nobody seems to know (who, whom) to call for information.

23. He (presently, currently) pitches for the Toledo Mudhens.

24. One thing (lead, led) to another.

25. She said she'd like to examine the issue (farther, further).

26. What does he think will be the (affect, effect) of the law?

27. That's not the way it's (suppose, supposed) to be.

28. I (use, used) to enjoy skiing until I broke my leg.

D. In the space before each number, put the letter of the sentence that is punctuated correctly.

1. ____ **a.** Fans at Sheridan, Westfield and Hamilton Heights supported the multiclass tournament.

   b. Fans at Sheridan, Westfield, and Hamilton Heights supported the multiclass tournament.

2. ____ **a.** Kansas City, Mo. is on the Kansas side of the state.

   b. Kansas City, Mo., is on the Kansas side of the state.

Basic Skills Pretest (Continued)

NAME: _____
CLASS: _____
DATE: _____

3. _____ **a.** Still, he was enthusiastic when three schools — Cherry Tree, Carmel Junior High and Carmel High School — applied for the Indiana 2000 grant.

　　b. Still, he was enthusiastic when three schools, Cherry Tree, Carmel Junior High, and Carmel High School, applied for the Indiana 2000 grant.

4. _____ **a.** Miller Co., Inc., and its employees have signed a new contract.

　　b. Miller Co. Inc. and its employees have signed a new contract.

5. _____ **a.** He said, "Our plate is pretty full with issues of rapid growth."

　　b. He said, "Our plate is pretty full with issues of rapid growth".

6. _____ **a.** He said two of his favorite movies — "Claire's Knee" and "Chloe in the Afternoon" — are by director, Eric Rohmer.

　　b. He said two of his favorite movies — "Claire's Knee" and "Chloe in the Afternoon" — are by director Eric Rohmer.

7. _____ **a.** The Fenders' daughter Rosa will be married in June and their other daughter, Vanessa, in July.

　　b. The Fenders' daughter, Rosa, will be married in June and their other daughter Vanessa in July.

8. _____ **a.** "Who's there?" she screamed.

　　b. "Who's there?", she screamed.

9. _____ **a.** The superintendent said: "We can't afford everything. We have to pick and choose."

　　b. The superintendent said, "We can't afford everything. We have to pick and choose."

10. _____ **a.** A large flowery couch sat on the front porch.

　　b. A large, flowery couch sat on the front porch.

11. _____ **a.** She said her courses made her a well-prepared job applicant.

　　b. She said her courses made her a well prepared job applicant.

12. ____ **a.** The 21-year-old pool has problems; and it could cost nearly half a million dollars to bring it up to state codes.

         b. The 21-year-old pool has problems, and it could cost nearly half a million dollars to bring it up to state codes.

13. ____ **a.** Shoemaker, however says she won't file suit.

         b. Shoemaker, however, says she won't file suit.

14. ____ **a.** Rain's in the forecast for the rest of the week, too.

         b. Rain's in the forecast for the rest of the week too.

15. ____ **a.** He said he didn't do it then, but should have.

         b. He said he didn't do it then but should have.

Copy-Editing Symbols

NAME: _____
CLASS: _____
DATE: _____

A. Use proper copy-editing symbols to make the requested changes.

1. Insert the letter *s* after the *n:* inert.
2. Insert the word *not* between these words: will always.
3. Delete the last *e* in the first word, and close the space as needed: employeee benefits.
4. Delete the second *e* from the end of the first word, and close the space as needed: employeee benefits.
5. Delete the word *very,* and close the space: not very tall.
6. Delete the extra *n,* and make this one word: cannnot.
7. Transpose the *s* and the second *e:* thees.
8. Transpose the abbreviation and year in this date: 67 A.D.
9. Abbreviate *United States* Army in this sentence.
10. Make this numeral a number written out: 17.
11. Mark this sentence — including the number in front of it — so that it will be indented as a paragraph.
12. Mark this sentence — including the number in front of it — so that it will become part of the same paragraph as No. 11.

B. Use copy-editing symbols to edit the following news brief for wire-service style and spelling, and to correct any other errors.

A Rio loma man bitten by a poisonus corral snake bit back.

Richard Douglass, 44, was wakling along United State Hiway Forty-Four near Rountree when he stopped to pick up something he thuoght he saw in the gras but a poisonous snate but hishand.

7

Douglass bit the snakes head off, then saved his own life by using the reptiles skin for a tournicut to to keep the venem from spreding.

Douglas ought to fully recover, because the venem's pread was stopped intime, said Susie Chavez, a spokesman for springfield Hospital.

Chapter 1: Grammar Basics

NAME: _____

CLASS: _____

DATE: _____

1. What are some of the differences between spoken and written English?

2. Why do journalists use traditional grammar rather than one of the newer grammars, such as structural or transformational?

3. Why is consistency such a concern in the publishing industry?

4. List the eight parts of speech.

5. What are the three verbals?

6. List at least five parts of a sentence.

7. What is the difference between the parts of speech and the parts of a sentence?

Chapter 2: Phrases, Clauses and Sentences

NAME: _____
CLASS: _____
DATE: _____

1. What do phrases, clauses and sentences have in common?

2. What's the difference between a phrase and a clause?

3. What's the difference between a clause and a sentence?

4. What are the two kinds of clauses?

5. What are the two kinds of dependent clauses?

6. What do the terms *restrictive* and *nonrestrictive* mean?

7. What's the difference between *that* and *which*?

8. What's the difference between *that* and *who*?

9. What are the four kinds of sentences classified by form?

10. Write a simple sentence.

11. Now, add a second thought to it in the form of an independent clause to make a compound sentence.

12. Next, go back to your original simple sentence and add a dependent clause to it to make a complex sentence.

13. Finally, combine your compound and complex sentences to make a single compound-complex one.

14. Write a complex sentence with a subordinate clause.

15. Now, write a complex sentence with a relative clause.

Chapter 2: Restrictive vs. Nonrestrictive

NAME: _____

CLASS: _____

DATE: _____

Use proper copy-editing symbols to insert or remove commas (if necessary) in the following sentences according to whether the modifiers are restrictive or nonrestrictive. Do not rewrite the sentences. If the context is not clear enough to determine the author's intended meaning, write a query.

1. Former University of Missouri student, Gloria Julow Gillis, will be the featured artist in an exhibition next week at the Columbia Art League.

2. Phyllis Tewes, whose family now lives in Bloomington, Ind. said her son will always remain special to her.

3. Before the operation was halted, bills surfaced at stores in Moscow and in Kiev where foreigners use American dollars, not Russian rubles.

4. That is my wife Susan over there.

5. From the corner, the third house that has a lawn jockey attacking a pink flamingo is mine.

6. Wilbur and Ann Bogdonovich announce the engagement of their daughter April to Mark Faber.

7. Stephen King's novel, "Cujo," sold well as usual for his books.

8. Margaret Mitchell's one novel "Gone With the Wind" has proved a favorite with readers.

9. John McLaughlin has played guitar in many genres of music. This album by him for example is jazz.

10. Filmmaker, Woody Allen, is one of my favorites.

11. Santa Claus with his packages will slide down the chimney tonight.

12. John Horner who is a playwright will be there.

13. This latest poem your best I think is a good example of what I mean.

14. This Hawaiian shirt which my son gave me is one of my favorites.

15. The ring, that his wife gave him when they married, has an inscription on the inside.

16. The program, that I saw last night, was excellent.

17. Shakespeare's well-known play, "The Merchant of Venice," is where we find the speech about "the quality of mercy."
18. The person who did that should be ashamed.
19. Don't drink the water unless you have a strong stomach.
20. The building, across the street, is the library.
21. John as well as Henry says he will attend.
22. There should be a comma according to what my teacher said before the word *too* at the end of a sentence.
23. I don't however believe him.
24. I'd like to, although, I don't think I can.
25. She, though disagreed.

Chapter 2: Sentence Errors

NAME: _____

CLASS: _____

DATE: _____

A. Label each of the following *S* for sentence, *FR* for fragment, *CS* for comma splice, *FU* for fused or *R* for run-on.

1. _____ I'm not going out with her.

2. _____ No matter how often she asks.

3. _____ Many people enjoyed "Twin Peaks," the ratings proved it.

4. _____ Leonard Cohen's songs are dark and moody, but Bob Dylan's are usually more cheerful, but sometimes he can be as obscure as Cohen, but then again, he's more surrealistic, whereas Cohen is surrealistic, too, but mainly just plain weird, although sometimes he's funny, too, like Dylan but not usually.

5. _____ Because I want to.

6. _____ That's what I'm going to do I'm going to talk to him.

7. _____ Stephenson's. Home of great apple pie.

8. _____ I don't know how people afford to live there the housing costs are so high.

9. _____ The computer works fine, so does the modem.

10. _____ That's how it goes, sometimes things disappear mysteriously around her.

B. Rewrite the following sentences to make them parallel in construction.

1. My favorite sports activities are playing soccer, Australian-rules football on television and to go to a baseball game.

2. First, read the introduction to each chapter, then you should complete the exercise.

3. Co-workers say the new boss is intelligent, friendly and he inspires them.

Chapter 3: Subjects and Objects: Nouns and Pronouns

NAME: _____

CLASS: _____

DATE: _____

1. What are the three cases of nouns and pronouns, and when do you use each?

2. What's the difference between a common noun and a proper noun?

3. What's the difference between intensive and reflexive pronouns?

4. What's the difference between *who* and *whom*, *whoever* and *whomever*?

Chapter 3: Common Nouns vs. Proper Nouns

NAME: _____
CLASS: _____
DATE: _____

A. Use proper copy-editing symbols to correct the following generic terms and brand names.

1. aqualung
2. astroturf
3. band-aid
4. dumpster
5. jeep
6. jello
7. kitty litter
8. laundromat
9. Naugahyde
10. novocain
11. realtor
12. rollerblade
13. Scotch tape
14. seeing-eye dog
15. styrofoam
16. velcro
17. Windbreaker
18. Xerox
19. ziplock

B. Use proper copy-editing symbols to correct the capitalization of the following names according to the rules for animals, foods and plants.

1. lily of the valley
2. Boston cream pie
3. German Shepherd
4. dutch elm
5. french fries
6. Red Delicious Apple
7. basset hound
8. Russian dressing
9. Bavarian Cream
10. swiss cheese
11. English Toffee
12. granny Smith apple
13. Italian Bread
14. manhattan cocktail
15. Waldorf Salad
16. Graham crackers
17. irish setter

Chapter 3: The Forms Nouns Take

NAME: _____

CLASS: _____

DATE: _____

A. Use proper copy-editing symbols to edit these sentences.

1. She said its not it's fault.

2. Who's book is this? Whose going to claim it?

3. Is this yours?

4. That car is their's.

5. Everybody's here.

6. The air is everybodys.

7. One's reputation cant be returned easily after its been taken away.

8. The preacher ended his prayer with "In Jesus's name, amen."

9. Is this where the Smith's live?

10. Is this the Smiths house?

11. This pizza belongs to the Joneses'.

12. This pizza is the Jones'.

13. The attorney generals decision is expected next month.

14. The attorneys general of most of the states met over the summer.

15. The cabin belongs to the sons-in-law jointly.

16. The two mothers-in-law's beliefs were at odds.

17. Fred and Edie's car was blue.

18. Bill and Henry's grades left something to be desired.

Chapter 3: The Forms Nouns Take (Continued)

NAME: _____
CLASS: _____
DATE: _____

19. The Wilsons are coming over for dinner tonight.

20. Whose been knocking at who's door?

21. Carla Fredericks is on her way to visit the rest of the Fredericks.

22. The Kellys are coming over tonight.

B. Use proper copy-editing symbols to add or delete apostrophes as needed.

1. baker's dozen
2. baker's yeast
3. boatmans holiday
4. children's theater
5. nurses aide
6. teachers college
7. teachers salaries
8. womens college
9. writers guide

Chapter 3: Pronoun Forms and Agreement

NAME: _____

CLASS: _____

DATE: _____

Use proper copy-editing symbols to edit the following sentences as needed for correct pronoun-antecedent agreement and for clear pronoun reference.

(Note: Later pronouns in any sentence here refer to antecedents in the sentence, not to someone else who's unspecified. For example, in No. 10, the pronoun in front of *song* refers to the person or people mentioned earlier, not to someone else.)

1. A reporter should check their copy before giving it to the city editor.
2. The City Council said they would consider the sewer issue at tonight's public hearing.
3. The committee will hold their next meeting Monday.
4. The Detroit Tigers will play their next game at home.
5. Everyone has had their ego bruised at one time or other.
6. All have done his part.
7. Everyone deserves to get his or her wish.
8. No one can accomplish anything unless they try.
9. Either he or they are going to sing their song next.
10. Either they or he is going to sing his song next.
11. Neither Bill nor Shirley would do their part.
12. Before she recommended the student, Young read his résumé.
13. It's raining outside.
14. As she stood before the audience at the assembly, she froze for a moment as she looked at their faces.
15. The jury had to consider their own conscience as well as the law.
16. After the game, the team went to their homes.
17. Each of the birds in the flock has their own personality.
18. The committee members are split in their political leanings.

25

19. The board voted for the ban under the gun of federal regulators, who threatened to cut funding if they didn't.

20. It's not known whether his brother and his wife were on the plane.

Chapter 3: Problems With Pronoun Case

NAME: _____

CLASS: _____

DATE: _____

Use proper copy-editing symbols to edit the pronouns in these sentences for correct pronoun case.

1. Between you and I, this looks easier than I thought.
2. Valerie was mistaken to be her. And they mistook her to be she.
3. For Joann and myself, good night.
4. Give the information to either Steve or I.
5. It's me!
6. Us journalism students have it bad but not so bad as them.
7. Hand it to him or myself.
8. Neither him nor her could make it.
9. They believed John to be me.
10. I thought she to be her. Jane was mistaken to be her.
11. We enjoyed him playing soccer.
12. The wrestler weighs 450 pounds. Can you imagine his falling on yourself?
13. They said they had thought it was her and me who went to the costume party as the "Love Boat."
14. You and I have much in common.
15. Would you hand these to he and she?
16. Andrew and myself went camping over the weekend.
17. Is Terry's husband older than her?
18. We hope Bill and her will visit soon.
19. They picked him to win the race.
20. Carol was assumed to be she in the window — wasn't it her?
21. Include a picture of yourself.

22. I, myself, think she's the person for the job.

23. I did it to save me time. To save myself money, I would have done something else.

24. Give one of these to whoever asks for one.

Chapter 3: Who vs. Whom, Whoever vs. Whomever; Chapter 2: That vs. Which

NAME: _____
CLASS: _____
DATE: _____

Use proper copy-editing symbols to edit the following sentences for the correct use of the relative pronouns *who*, *whom*, *whoever*, *whomever*, *that* and *which*.

1. The cannon belongs to the Mayflower Hotel, who is one of the organizers of the rally.
2. It's a mistake to give your credit-card number to whoever asks for it over the phone.
3. Who are you talking to?
4. Give one of these to whoever asks for one.
5. Who did the City Council appoint to the post?
6. Nobody seems to know who to call for information.
7. The deputies which the sheriff chastised refused to comment.
8. The victim, that was identified as Will Beason, was a drifter.
9. Did she say who we would be reading in this course?
10. Collect the money from whomever will pay it.
11. Whomever would have thought it would be Atlanta!
12. Whoever is going should line up here.
13. Who are you going to try to get to play the organ this week at church?
14. Whom was it who played bass in Jim Morrison's band?
15. By who was this painted?
16. The impersonator can imitate whoever you want him to be.
17. The animals who need protecting most are put on the endangered species list.
18. The fish who got away may be the one which old-timers call "Big Wally."
19. The books which interest me the most are classics.
20. Bill Seraphim, the hospital president, told the board Monday that Wyandotte Health Services, who is leasing the hospital, has plans to solve the space shortage.

21. That's the particle whose characteristics we are studying.

22. The jetliner which crashed in the mountains near Grand Junction, Colo., was headed for Los Angeles. The plane, that was carrying 83 passengers, had radioed it was having engine trouble.

Chapter 4: Subject-Verb Agreement

NAME: _____
CLASS: _____
DATE: _____

For pronoun-antecedent agreement and subject-predicate agreement, it's essential to be able to recognize whether a noun or pronoun is singular or plural. Indefinite pronouns and foreign, collective and uncountable nouns cause many people problems.

For each of the following, put an *S* in front of the word if it is always singular, *P* if it is always plural or *SP* if it can be either one depending on context. In the case of collective nouns, which only occasionally vary according to context, indicate what they would *normally* be.

1. _____ all
2. _____ alumni
3. _____ anybody
4. _____ athletics
5. _____ bacteria
6. _____ commission
7. _____ corporation
8. _____ council
9. _____ couple
10. _____ criteria
11. _____ data
12. _____ each
13. _____ either
14. _____ ethics
15. _____ everyone
16. _____ faculty
17. _____ few
18. _____ jury
19. _____ little
20. _____ mathematics
21. _____ measles
22. _____ media
23. _____ most
24. _____ mumps
25. _____ neither
26. _____ news
27. _____ no one
28. _____ nothing
29. _____ one
30. _____ oxen
31. _____ panel
32. _____ phenomenon
33. _____ pliers
34. _____ politics
35. _____ remainder
36. _____ scissors
37. _____ several
38. _____ some
39. _____ what

Chapter 4: Subject-Verb Agreement, No. 1

NAME: _____

CLASS: _____

DATE: _____

Use proper copy-editing symbols to edit the following sentences for subject-predicate agreement.

1. The panel are Betty, Bill and Joan. Betty, Bill and Joan is the panel.
2. Alan and Henry are going. Alan, as well as Henry, is going.
3. No one but they knows the answer.
4. Here comes the Wilsons!
5. There's three nevers in comedy.
6. Out of the book comes three ideas.
7. The committee is agreed. The committee are disagreed.
8. Measles are seldom fatal.
9. The media is not to blame for bad news.
10. The number of people are small. A total of 30 is going.
11. None of the local dealers was there. None of them agree about what should be done.
12. Each is going by car. They are each going by car.
13. The Sufi sage said the evils of the world is what God permits to thicken the plot.
14. Only one of the 12 professors seems interesting.
15. Pork and beans is a favorite Western dish.
16. Here's two rules you shouldn't forget.
17. There's a few of them now.
18. The committee are Letisha, Brian and Rosa.
19. The jury disagree on a verdict.
20. Mashed potatoes and gravy are a favorite dish with steak.

Chapter 4: Subject-Verb Agreement, No. 2

NAME: _____

CLASS: _____

DATE: _____

B. Use proper copy-editing symbols to edit the following sentences for subject-predicate agreement.

1. Each of them are going by car.
2. Only one of the 20 have agreed.
3. He, as well as they, know the hidden message.
4. Ben, as well as Juanita, are going.
5. You, as well as they, know the hidden message.
6. The state of Missouri is one of those that has filed legal opposition to Clark's ruling.
7. The media was there to cover the accident even before the ambulance arrived.
8. The committee were split over the amendment.
9. A number of researchers was shocked by the report.
10. Lin is one of the girls who were nominated.
11. None of us were invited.
12. There aren't enough data.
13. Here's a few of the books you requested.
14. What he ordered were computer disks.
15. Physicists now think of atomic particles as something that pops in and out of existence according to chance.
16. The radio said 1 to 3 inches of snow is possible.
17. One-third of the students is from out of state.
18. She said she hopes for a cure for AIDS as a team of testers search.
19. Peas and carrots are not his favorite vegetable dish.

Chapter 5: Verbs

NAME: _____

CLASS: _____

DATE: _____

1. What's the difference between a *transitive* verb and an *intransitive* verb?

2. What are the two kinds of intransitive verbs?

3. List the principal parts of the verb *to lie* (recline).

4. Conjugate the verb *to raise* in all six tenses. Label the tenses.

5. Conjugate the verb *to write* in third-person singular for all six progressive forms. Label each form.

6. Define passive voice, and list its three characteristics.

7. List the names of the four moods of a verb, and tell how each is used.

8. Conjugate the verb *to sing* in all its imperative-mood forms.

9. List the indicative and conditional forms of the helping verbs that change form in the conditional.

10. How is the subjunctive mood formed for all verbs other than *to be?*

11. Conjugate the verb *to be* in the present and past subjunctive.

Chapter 5: Tenses, No. 1

NAME: _____
CLASS: _____
DATE: _____

List the four principal parts of the following verbs.

1. awake

2. bring

3. broadcast

4. burst

5. dive

6. drink

7. drown

8. forbid

39

9. get

10. hang (execute)

11. hang (suspend)

12. hide

13. lay

14. lie (recline)

15. pay

16. plead

17. prove

18. raise

Chapter 5: Tenses, No. 1 (Continued)

NAME: _____
CLASS: _____
DATE: _____

19. rise

20. set

21. shine

22. sit

23. steal

24. swear

25. swim

Chapter 5: Tenses, No. 2

NAME: _____

CLASS: _____

DATE: _____

Circle the *correct* answers.

1. "I think he's (prejudice, prejudiced)," she said.

2. I (use, used) to jog but gave it up.

3. These parts aren't fitting together as they're (suppose, supposed) to do.

4. I think I'll go (lay, lie) down.

5. For several days, he just (lay, laid, lied) around, doing nothing.

6. (Sit, set) the bag of cement down over there.

7. Don't (sit, set) down until the concrete in the walk has had a chance to (set, sit).

8. The lake level is (raising, rising) higher than it has in the past.

9. (Raise, Rise) up for a minute, will you?

10. Has your new job (brought, brung) you any happiness?

11. I had (got, gotten) up early that morning.

12. They (hanged, hung) the condemned man at midnight.

13. She said she (is, was) smarter than that now.

14. When my back has been hurting, sometimes I've (laid, lain, lied) down on the floor at home.

15. I had just (sat, satted, set, setted) down when the phone rang.

16. When she came home from work, she found that her husband had (hanged, hung) all the pictures in their new home.

17. The defendant (pleaded, pled) guilty.

18. A 3-year-old Mayfield child (drown, drowned, drowneded) Wednesday in a pond behind her home. A neighbor saw her fall in and (dived, dove) in after her but was too late.

19. Do you remember the date "A Prairie Home Companion" was first (broadcast, broadcasted)?

20. When they came home from visiting their grandparents over Christmas, they found their water pipes had frozen and (burst, bust, bursted, busted).

21. When's the next time we get (paid, payed)?

22. I know I (lay, laid, layed) those keys down somewhere!

23. One thing (lead, led) to another.

24. Professor Ian Hathaway said the moon (is, was) a satellite.

Chapter 5: Voice

NAME: _____

CLASS: _____

DATE: _____

A. Put a check beside each sentence with a passive-voice verb.

1. _____ The story was edited by the copy desk.
2. _____ The copy desk has edited the story.
3. _____ The story was edited.
4. _____ Was this story edited?
5. _____ Has anyone edited this story?
6. _____ Has this story been edited?
7. _____ The medicine has been proved to be effective.
8. _____ The medicine is proven effective.
9. _____ He burned the toast.
10. _____ The toast was burned.
11. _____ The toast was burnt.
12. _____ I was lost.
13. _____ Too many assignments were due at once.
14. _____ I felt I was treated unfairly.
15. _____ The president was elected in a landslide.
16. _____ The cat was not harmed by the experience.
17. _____ The professor was acting pretty strangely.
18. _____ His birthday was celebrated in St. Louis.
19. _____ The commissioner was arrested for tax evasion.
20. _____ Police said the man was shot several times in the chest.
21. _____ The police were searching for more evidence.
22. _____ The evidence was gathered over the weekend.
23. _____ The exam was given promptly at noon.
24. _____ The man shot the mayor.

25. _____ The bills were due.

26. _____ It was hard for him to see in the dark room.

27. _____ The noise was deafening.

28. _____ The election was held in secret.

29. _____ The sun was shining.

B. Improve the following sentences, where possible, by rewriting them in active voice.

1. Damage to the house and its contents was estimated by the Fire Department to be about $200,000.

2. Police said no one was seen leaving the building.

3. The fire investigator said no evidence of arson was found.

4. The downtown First National Bank was robbed this morning of about $25,000 by a man wearing a Halloween mask of President Clinton.

5. Sam Smothers, 28, of Ashland was killed when the car he was driving was struck by a pickup heading north on U.S. 63.

6. No charges have been filed.

7. A good time was had by all.

Chapter 5: Mood

NAME: _____

CLASS: _____

DATE: _____

A. Circle the *correct* answers.

1. I wouldn't if I (was, were) you.
2. She moved that the resolution (be, is) approved.
3. He demanded that the committee (decide, decides) now.
4. If he (sing, sings), will you attend?
5. If she (was, were) coming, she'd be here by now.
6. He plays piano as though he (was, were) a professional.
7. When someone sneezes, we say, "God (bless, blesses) you."
8. If she (be, is) guilty, she should go to prison.
9. I wish I (was, were) through with this assignment.
10. If I hurt your feelings, I (am, be) sorry.
11. He said he could do the job better if he (had, has, have) better tools.
12. If this (be, is) what I think it (be, is), then it (be, is) an important finding.
13. His mom insisted that he (stay, stays) home and (help, helps) with the dishes.
14. I prefer that you (go, goes).
15. They recommended he (take, takes) more classes in English.
16. I might do it if I (was, were) asked.
17. We only ask that she (finish, finishes) the assignment.
18. I (am, be) happy.
19. It's necessary I (am, be) left alone.

B. Use proper copy-editing symbols to correct these sentences for verb mood where necessary.

1. If I was going to go, I'd have dressed by now.
2. If he is guilty, he should hang.

3. If he was any taller, we'd have to raise the ceiling.

4. If he edit this by tomorrow, will you reconsider lowering his grade?

5. I demand that she stays.

6. I insist he goes.

7. I suppose that you be right.

8. Lest he forget, I shall remind him.

9. First, read the introduction to each chapter, then you should complete the exercise.

10. If the new policy is not overturned by the courts, companies will be required to have programs in place by December.

Chapter 5: Nouns Used as Verbs

NAME: _____

CLASS: _____

DATE: _____

In the following sentences, substitute other verbs for any that were formed from nouns and that editors frequently find objectionable. We've also thrown in two verbs used improperly as nouns; try to find them, too.

1. For more information about hosting a Tupperware party, contact Belinda Hamilton at 555-8212.

2. The movie, targeted at a younger audience, premieres Thursday.

3. William Least Heat-Moon authored the popular "Blue Highways" and also penned a second book.

4. The people of the village gifted me with this necklace.

5. Let's interface next week and ink a contract.

6. The Institute for Objectivist Studies is headquartered in Poughkeepsie, N.Y.

7. The director said she needs to process a few script changes before the production is ready to debut.

8. None of our neighbors jet off to the Bahamas for the weekend!

9. He read a book to learn how to parent his daughter better.

10. We need someone strong to chairman the committee.

11. They'll take a win wherever they can find one.

12. There seemed to be a big disconnect between the media and the American public over the Clinton scandal.

Chapter 6: Modifiers

NAME: _____

CLASS: _____

DATE: _____

1. What characteristics do adjectives and adverbs share?

2. Name the three degrees of comparison, and explain how to form them — first for adjectives, then for adverbs.

3. Define and give the two characteristics of coordinate adjectives.

4. How should coordinate adjectives be punctuated?

5. What two common kinds of adjectives are we not considering coordinate adjectives?

6. What is a compound modifier?

7. How should compound modifiers be punctuated when they precede the word they modify? What are the common exceptions?

8. What is an article? What part of speech is it?

9. What are three things that adverbs tend to tell us?

10. What is a sentence adverb? What sentence adverb is most likely to get you in trouble?

11. Should adverbs ever come between the parts of a verb phrase?

12. We're calling interjections modifiers because they often resemble what?

13. Which two kinds of verbals are often used as modifiers?

14. How can you tell the difference between a participle used in forming a passive-voice verb and a participle used as a predicate adjective?

15. What is a dangling participle? A nominative absolute?

Chapter 6: Comparative Forms of Adjectives and Adverbs

NAME: _____
CLASS: _____
DATE: _____

A. List the three degrees of comparison for each of these adjectives.

1. bad

2. beautiful

3. big

4. dark

5. easy

6. famous

7. far

8. fast

9. good

53

10. little

11. many

12. old

B. List the three degrees of comparison for each of these adverbs.

  1. badly

  2. carefully

  3. fast

  4. likely

  5. quickly

  6. soon

  7. well

Chapter 6: Comparative Forms of Adjectives and Adverbs (Continued)

NAME: _____

CLASS: _____

DATE: _____

C. Edit these sentences for the proper degree of comparison and any other problems of meaning, such as inclusiveness and double negatives.

1. He is the older of the three editors and has one of the more unique book collections I've ever seen.

2. Hopefully, it won't snow over Thanksgiving break.

3. She is the youngest of the two sisters.

4. The winning driver was faster than anyone in the race.

5. More important, this brand of computer costs less.

6. That doesn't hardly ever happen.

7. He said he hasn't smoked but once.

8. He was the taller of all the other players on the basketball team.

9. Because of the smoke, you can't hardly see the mountains some days.

10. The new professor we've hired has more years in the field than anyone on the faculty.

11. Which of these two cars do you think is best?

12. Most all of them are ready.

Chapter 6: Adjectives vs. Adverbs

NAME: _____

CLASS: _____

DATE: _____

Use proper copy-editing symbols to edit the following sentences for correct use of adjectives and adverbs.

1. This brew goes down smoother than that one.
2. The car was traveling quick. The bus was also moving fast.
3. I finished slower than most.
4. Flowers smell sweetly this time of year.
5. I feel badly about that.
6. The car ran good after the tuneup.
7. The new father looked proudly as he left the hospital.
8. She hit her brakes quicker than the other driver.
9. At that question, Jimenez waxed philosophically.
10. I don't feel well today.
11. The parking meters were checked regular.
12. He did good on the final exam.
13. The new typesetter is working real well.
14. He kicked the ball past the goalie perfect.
15. When the monk rang the bell, it sounded out loud.
16. It looked to me that he was playing too cautious for that field position.
17. The music sounded loud even though it was coming from the next building.
18. The pickles taste rather sourly.
19. She's performing rather weak in that role.
20. Turn the dial slow, or you'll go right past the station.
21. Firstly, let's consider our options.

22. I'm going to start having to eat more healthy.

23. Write it right.

24. We drove real slowly through the fog.

Chapter 6: Coordinate Adjectives vs. Compound Modifiers

NAME: _____
CLASS: _____
DATE: _____

Use proper copy-editing symbols to insert commas or hyphens where needed in the following sentences.

1. The short pudgy man wearing a gardenia is I.

2. The part time worker is well liked.

3. The tall thin gentleman is my uncle.

4. The story about the old yellow dog is a sad one.

5. She is a part time worker. He works part time.

6. He's old fashioned but well liked.

7. The 36 year old man moved here four years ago.

8. Shelter Insurance is a mutual multiple lines company.

9. The spotted black dog bit the happy looking man.

10. She remembers it as a dark terrible night.

11. He was given a five to 10 year prison sentence.

12. Although the short term problems of the drought, such as loss of topsoil moisture and lack of water in farm ponds, could be corrected with 3 to 5 inches of rain, the extension agent said long term problems will be more serious.

13. Small business incomes declined 3 percent in March.

14. The three planks were each 6 foot long boards.

15. The partially completed work has not been touched in years.

16. She is a well respected poet, translator and editor.

17. The Saturday afternoon football game was played under a light blue sky.

18. The suspect in the child sex abuse case was originally arrested on a charge of armed criminal action.

19. The real estate agent decided she should get a blood pressure check.

20. Norton said he favored a gasoline tax increase to fund the $100 million project.

21. The game's most valuable player spent the summer working in a walk in storage facility.

22. Some poets prefer a four foot poetic line.

Chapter 6: Articles

NAME: _____

CLASS: _____

DATE: _____

Use proper copy-editing symbols to edit the following sentences for issues involving articles. Some of the sentences involve usage issues for which you should consult Chapter 8.

1. The higher education commissioner finds herself in an unique situation.

2. This is a historic occasion.

3. We've got a half hour before the concert starts.

4. Do you have a couple minutes?

5. I'd say it's kind of a break.

6. Alot of people would agree.

7. I haven't seen her for awhile.

8. The alarm rang just a while ago.

9. He holds an honorary doctorate from Tulane University.

10. It's a whole nother world out there!

Chapter 6: Dangling Participles and Misplaced Modifiers

NAME: _____
CLASS: _____
DATE: _____

Rewrite the following sentences, as needed, to fix awkward modifier placement and to clarify meaning. If a sentence could have more than one meaning, pick the more probable and rewrite accordingly. Also, query intent where you think it is necessary to do so.

1. Hanging from the cave ceiling, he saw thousands of bats.

2. However, it hasn't happened yet.

3. Going back for the fly ball, the sun got in his eyes.

4. The computer having gone down, the paper was late.

5. The award was developed after Robert Kennedy was assassinated by a group of journalists he traveled with during his presidential campaign in 1968.

6. Johnson only has one of the rare baseball cards.

7. I just want to quickly end this dispute.

8. The clock has been consistently gaining time.

9. To get ahead in the music business, the audience must be kept in mind. And they must enjoy you playing.

10. Seeing them again, it was as though it were 20 years ago.

11. She wants to not be disturbed.

12. As a psychologist, a lot of our viewers may wonder what your connection is to sports.

13. Cleaned and crushed, distributors send the cans to aluminum recycling plants.

14. Knowing that a dog won't eat what he can't smell, which dog food would you buy?

15. The Rev. Jesse Jackson was greeted by 2,000 mostly black supporters.

16. Phil Barnsworth said he wants to be "the jobs mayor" Friday.

17. Two men — one carrying a bomb and the other an officer of the New Jewish Defense League — were arrested on charges of plotting to bomb an Arab tourist office.

18. People who work slowly adjust to the grind.

19. The Screen Actors Guild had been, for more than two months, picketing the studios.

20. After winning the race, a drug test stripped away his gold medal.

Chapter 7: Connecting Words

NAME: _____
CLASS: _____
DATE: _____

1. What's an easy way to recognize most prepositions?

2. What things do prepositions tell us?

3. What do prepositions connect?

4. Prepositional phrases are used in place of what parts of speech?

5. What should you do if you find a sentence (not in a quotation) ending in a preposition?

6. What are the differences between coordinate conjunctions and subordinate conjunctions?

7. What are the differences between conjunctions and conjunctive adverbs?

8. What's the difference between a conjunction and a relative pronoun?

Chapter 7: Connecting Words, No. 2

NAME: _____
CLASS: _____
DATE: _____

Circle the *correct* answers. To fix some of these, you might need to consult your stylebook and Chapter 8 of *Working With Words*.

1. The issue (centers around, centers on) the vice president's image.

2. (Prior to, Before) the operation, she was in constant pain.

3. Neither the alumni (or, nor) the students seem to favor the proposal.

4. His vase was different (from, than) the one at the museum; compared (to, with) his, the museum's looked plain.

5. The tests found the dog was free (from, of) disease.

6. She was wearing a dress identical (to, with) mine!

7. Police investigated the business (in which he was involved, in which he was involved in) for mob connections.

8. This exercise is (to, too, two) easy.

9. He thought the shirt wasn't made (as, so) well as the ones he buys through the mail.

10. I don't know (if, whether, whether or not) I want to go.

11. (While, Although) we disagreed at the time with what he said, we later decided he made some good points.

12. (Among, Between) the three of us, we can probably put together a proposal that will compare favorably (to, with) theirs.

13. (Among, Between) the two of us, we should try to help (each other, one another).

14. She was convicted (of, with) soliciting.

15. Not only he (also, but also, in addition) she agreed.

16. He was (convinced, persuaded) that he should try to (convince, persuade) others to go to the seminar.

17. The administration said they were (forbidden, prohibited) from protesting.

To the left of each number, put the letter of the grammatically preferable wording or word break.

1. _____ **a.** He's the boy I'd like to give my baseball glove to.

b. He's the boy to whom I'd like to give my baseball glove.

2. _____ **a.** City to Look
Into Corruption Charges

b. City to Look Into
Corruption Charges

3. _____ **a.** He thought this exercise the hardest because there were so many unrelated points to remember.

b. He thought this exercise the hardest, because there were so many unrelated points to remember.

Chapter 8: Usage: Distinctions Made by Wire Services

NAME: _____
CLASS: _____
DATE: _____

Circle the *correct* answers. These are all usage distinctions mady by the wire services.

1. I want to watch that new show (that, which) gets (under way, underway) on (television, TV) tonight.

2. (Who, Whom) do you know at the United Nations (that, who) drinks Scotch (whiskey, whisky)?

3. The 8th U.S. Circuit Court of Appeals will hear the case involving the U.S. (Post Office, Postal Service) and the (U.S. Weather Bureau, National Weather Service).

4. The low Friday was (−10 degrees F., minus 10, 10 below, 10 below 0 Fahrenheit).

5. (Whose, Who's) book is this?

6. A verbal report (is an oral one, is a written one, may be oral or written).

7. *Presently* means (now, soon).

8. I can't (accept, except) the (affect, effect) the authors say they found.

9. At the air show, the group passed out a (flier, flyer) about a famous squadron of (fliers, flyers).

10. She had (blond, blonde) hair for (a while, awhile) until she became (convinced, persuaded) of the beauty of her natural color.

11. The department has $4 million in its budget this year, compared (to, with) $4.2 million last year, yet the need for its services among county (citizens, residents) is no different (from, than) what it was last year.

12. The 19-year-old (boy, man) (collided with, hit) a parked car when the gear jumped into reverse and his truck hurdled (backward, backwards).

13. He said she should look into the cult (farther, further), but that didn't (faze, phase) her.

14. Her friends will (hold, host) the party to raise money for a campaign to (hike, increase) the social services budget.

15. Let's discuss this (among, between) the three of us.

16. A female graduate of a college is an (alumnus, alumna, alumnae, alumni).

17. We need to drive 3 miles (farther, further).

18. The female suspect had (brunet, brunette) hair.

Chapter 8: Substantives and Verbs

NAME: _____

CLASS: _____

DATE: _____

Circle the *correct* answers.

1. The Lugnuts are a minor league baseball team in Lansing, the state (capital, Capitol).

2. A tanker spill could affect all (citizens, residents) within a radius of several miles.

3. A prisoner who is released early is out on (parole, probation); a person who is sentenced but not sent to jail is out on (parole, probation).

4. What's your (alibi, excuse) for missing the test?

5. One of the stars of "Gilligan's Island," she is an (alumna, alumnae, alumni, alumnus) of Stephens College.

6. How many (carats, carets, carrots, karats, karates) is that diamond?

7. Why don't villains in soap operas ever get their just (deserts, desserts)?

8. All (discs, disks) are (discs, disks), but not all (discs, disks) are (discs, disks).

9. William is interested in insects. He's an (entomologist, etymologist).

10. A (palate, palette, pallet) is the roof of the mouth. A (palate, palette, pallet) is a board on which an artist mixes paints. A (palate, palette, pallet) is a small, hard bed.

11. About 300 (people, persons) showed up.

12. That price represents a real (saving, savings)!

13. We enjoyed the (trek, trip) to the convention.

14. The law does not permit discrimination against people on the basis of (gender, sex).

15. The town was subjected to (rack, wrack, wreck) and ruin.

16. The president's (aid, aide) said he had not been told otherwise.

17. The farm bill was (adopted, approved, passed) by the Kansas Legislature.

18. Yesterday, I was so tired I (laid, lay, layed, lain) down on my couch and went to sleep.

19. He had just (laid, lay, layed, lain) down when the phone (rang, rung).

20. Would you (lend, loan) me your home computer to write my term paper?

21. To (assure, ensure, insure) we don't take too big a loss, we will (assure, ensure, insure) the shipment, I (assure, ensure, insure) you.

22. Fifty states (compose, comprise, constitute) the United States. Each state (comprises, is comprised of) many counties.

23. A speaker or writer (implies, infers); a listener or reader (implies, infers).

24. She (convinced, persuaded) him that he should try to (convince, persuade) his friends to attend.

25. The administration said they were (forbidden, prohibited) from protesting.

26. The spokesman said the government (anticipates, expects) enemy troop movements along the border.

27. When he slept through the alarm without (arousing, rousing), she decided to wake him.

28. At the '60s party, we'll be tie-(dieing, dying, dyeing) T-shirts.

29. They decided to (flaunt, flout) the law by (flaunting, flouting) their armbands.

30. We'd better (marshal, marshall, martial) our arguments before we go into that meeting.

31. Janet was (poring, pouring) over a book when I arrived.

32. First, you (flounder, founder), then you (flounder, founder).

33. The New Zealanders (gibed, jibed) the Australians because the protective skirt around their ship's hull didn't (gibe, jibe) with the sailors' idea of manliness.

34. (Set, Sit) the box down over here, please.

35. The terrorists (hanged, hung) one of their hostages Friday.

Chapter 8: Modifiers and Connectives

NAME: _____

CLASS: _____

DATE: _____

Circle the *correct* answers.

1. The flags at City Hall were lowered to (half-staff, half-mast), and the ceremony was (underway, under way).

2. To talk with someone (farther, further) about this, you're going to have to travel a few miles (farther, further).

3. Joan was feeling (eager, anxious) and was (eager, anxious) to get help from a psychotherapist.

4. For the (last, latest, past) 10 years, she said, she's been working on her magnum opus.

5. He was (amused, bemused, confused) by his friend's dry wit and smiled slightly.

6. A person who isn't married is (celibate, chaste); that doesn't mean, however, the person is (celibate, chaste).

7. The (enormity, enormousness) of the Nazi crimes cannot be forgiven.

8. I made it (especially, specially) for you.

9. Judging by the meaning of the words in the title, the book "The Sensuous Woman" would appear to be about (a woman who enjoys sex, a woman's senses of perception).

10. I'll meet you in (a half, half an) hour.

11. Springfield is considering a new (sewage, sewerage) system to handle its (sewage, sewerage) problems.

12. It was a (grisly, gristly, grizzly, grizzled) sight.

13. The desert was (continual, continuous) as far as the eye could see.

14. She thought his manner (aggravating, annoying, irritating).

15. The figures look different (from, than) last year's.

16. Compared (to, with) learning AP style, grammar may be easier.

17. He didn't say (if, whether, whether or not) there would be a quiz today.

18. (While, Although) the councilman opposed the motion in 1996, his wife, the mayor, voted for it in 1997.

19. (Among, Between) you, Fred and Steve, someone ought to be able to figure it out. Then you should share the information with (each other, one another).

20. The campaign (centers around, centers on) civic pride.

21. (Prior to, Before) coming here, I worked in Colorado.

22. There were (more than, over) 500 students registered.

23. I'll try (and, in, to) be done in 15 minutes.

24. (As, Like) I was saying, it's been a long time.

Chapter 8: Assorted Usage Problems

NAME: _____
CLASS: _____
DATE: _____

Circle the *correct* answers.

1. (Fewer, Less) people attended than the (fliers, flyers) handed out promised.

2. (I hope, Hopefully,) there won't be a blizzard during Thanksgiving vacation (as, like, such as) there usually is.

3. The convicted mass murderer was (hanged, hung) at one minute (passed, past) midnight.

4. (We, Us) philosophy students have it rough, but not (as, so) rough as (they, them).

5. She has (blond, blonde) hair, but her sister is a (brunet, brunette).

6. Mark Twain's house is (a, an) (historic, historical) (cite, sight, site).

7. (A lot, Quite a few, Many) of (us, we) residents were upset when we weren't (contacted, told) about the danger.

8. If I (was, were) (her, she), I'd be upset, too.

9. (More important, More importantly), we didn't know it was (he, him) when the doorbell rang.

10. We figured that the school's (principle, principal) was our (principle, principal) hope in the (stationary, stationery)-run endurance contest.

11. Research has (proved, proven) it: A usage exercise (as, like, such as) this one can help you sharpen your understanding of the differences (between, among) words.

12. The question remains: (What, what) (affect, effect) will the summit impasse have on hopes for an arms deal?

13. Finding a stone (auger, augur) does not (auger, augur) well for the professor's theory that this area was uninhabited until recently.

14. Inhabitants of (Britain, Briton) are (Britains, Britons).

15. He is as (callous, callus) as the (callouses, calluses) on his hands.

16. A body that's buried is (interred, interned); (interment, internment) refers to detainment.

17. She's (presently, currently) employed by Time and is expecting a big pay (hike, increase).

18. Put the ship and the (naval, navel) document over the (mantel, mantle).

19. They didn't sign a contract; they just made (a, an) (oral, verbal) agreement.

20. I'm (loath, loathe) to say it, but I (loath, loathe) that kind of music.

21. He's a (gourmand, gourmet), not a (gourmand, gourmet). Just (set, sit) food before him, and he'll eat it!

22. The smell from the (grill, grille) where they were cooking (hoards, hordes) of fish made me (nauseated, nauseous).

23. I was (reluctant, reticent) to say it, but I was (reluctant, reticent) to go to the rally (because, since, due to the fact that) I didn't know anyone.

24. Remember, (choose, chose) and (loose, lose) (rhyme, rhymes).

25. The workers let the (cement, concrete) walkway (set, sit) overnight.

26. (Every day, Everyday), (every one, everyone) should try to do (her, his, his or her, their) best.

27. The (affect, effect) was (masterful, masterly). She (elicited, illicited) the details of the (elicit, illicit) dealings from the (eminent, immanent, imminent) author.

28. The (premier, premiere) is the (premier, premiere) head of state in Europe.

29. When a loved one has died just before Christmas, it's difficult to enjoy the holiday. But over time, Christmas will become less (forbidding, foreboding) again.

30. What will the (affect, effect) be? How will this (affect, effect) us?

31. (A lot, Alot, Allot) of us don't know (what he's doing that for, why he's doing that).

32. Twenty appointees (compose, comprise, constitute) the task force.

33. (Farther, Further) down the road is a gasoline station.

Chapter 9: Punctuation

NAME: _____

CLASS: _____

DATE: _____

Use proper copy-editing symbols to fix punctuation and other errors in the following sentences as needed. Do not rewrite the sentences.

1. Who directed "Return of the Jedi?"

2. Three of her favorite books were "Atlas Shrugged" "Walden", and "Who's Afraid of Virginia Woolf"?

3. Robert Jones, Jr., has worked for Pioneer Foods, Inc. in Carthage Ill. since May 5, 1989 when he substituted for his brother.

4. They have lived in Independence, Kan., Leon, Iowa, and Boulder, Colo.

5. "If it weren't for this teams fighting spirit we wouldn't be No. 1", the coach said.

6. He said, "The U.S. didn't invade Nicaragua then, but should have. Then we wouldn't be in this mess in Central America today!!!"

7. Suddenly he sprang into action hitting one guard, kicking another, and tripping a third.

8. I don't want to; and that's final.

9. Stir and let set overnight.

10. I'd like that one too.

11. The story about the old, yellow dog is a sad one.

12. Her husband Bill was arrested for drunken driving.

13. Linda as well as Luis is going and I am too.

14. Davies hit the brakes, but couldn't avoid the car.

15. Wong suggested the way to deal with the drug problem was by, "teaching our children early of the dangers."

16. On Friday at Blue Ridge Elementary School a dentist and his staff discussed dental care and teachers used Mr. Gross Mouth to illustrate their points.

17. "The No. 1 problem we're facing is the lack of sufficient state funding", said the dean of the journalism program.

18. Soccer is the most popular sport in most of the world; but it hasn't caught on much in the United States.

19. Add 1 cup of water and stir for 5 minutes.

20. She loves Thomas Lux's poetry, and enjoys that of Larry Levis also.

21. The completely dull party was a disaster.

Chapter 9: Punctuating Quotations and Paraphrases

NAME: _____
CLASS: _____
DATE: _____

This exercise applies material from throughout the chapter that has to do with the handling of quotations. Use proper copy-editing symbols to fix the punctuation. If fixing some problems would require knowing the intended meaning of the reporter, query those items.

1. "My face is still slightly swollen after my face lift two weeks ago", she said, "but my doctor says that is normal and I can get my hair done next week."

2. When he graduates in May, Snodgrass says he does not know exactly what he will do.

3. None of the workers required medical treatment, and the leak did not pose a danger to public safety, he said.

4. Ramirez said he was "happy to be alive.

    "I can't believe it happened."

5. Hivala said the tribute and activities are for all veterans but its focus is on those in hospitals.

6. The mediator said he would explore the possibility of the Post's staff buying the paper, but said the limited time would make that difficult.

7. "That's a tough call," the coach said. "Let's wait till we see how the next game goes before we start predicting a championship."

    "But I'll tell you this, he added, "I'll be disappointed if we don't take home the trophy."

8. She said she thought her daughter was innocent but she was not so certain Strickland was blameless.

9. Hacker said about 7,500 deaths in Missouri each year are caused by smoking, and passage of a state law providing clean air indoors is vital for improving public health.

10. The poll found seven out of 10 people in the country support the proposal, and another two out of 10 are undecided.

11. Steger said the two communist countries will provide financial and logistical aid, and each will be represented by a member on the six-man expedition crew.

12. He said he didn't want to do it, but would try.

13. Next year, Jean-Louis Renaut, 23, said that he will return to teach in a "lycée" in France, and will also head up a program to encourage international travel abroad.

14. The researcher said, "We don't think we'll have a cure next week, but we do think this new study could mean a cure sometime down the road. In the meantime, though, I'm afraid a lot of people will suffer."

15. "Why wait till we graduate," asked the student?

16. "Wow!", she said. "I didn't know that."

17. "I think it was the poet Mark Strand who said, "The future isn't what it used to be." the professor said.

18. "Is that so"?, he said.

19. "I never saw anything like it in my life. And I hope I never do again," she said.

20. "Have you ever read James Joyce's "Ulysses?"," she asked.

Chapter 10: Spelling Relief

NAME: _____

CLASS: _____

DATE: _____

1. To check the spelling of a word, what three books should you consult? List them in the order they should be consulted.

2. What is the rule for the order of the letters *i* and *e* in a word?

3. What is the rule for when we typically double the consonant at the end of a word before adding a suffix that starts with a vowel?

4. Use proper copy-editing symbols to correct any misspelled words.

   accommodate

   advisor

   batallion

   cancellation

   cemetary

   compatible

   concensus

   defendant

   dietician

   disassociate

   donut

   embarass

   employe

exaggerate

fulfill

guerilla

harass

homocide

inocuous

judgment

kidnapped

livable

midieval

miniscule

momento

occassion

occured

restauranteur

seperate

sieze

supercede

superintendant

traveled

weird

Chapter 10: One Word, Two Words or Hyphenated? A-M

NAME: _____
CLASS: _____
DATE: _____

Use proper copy-editing symbols to correct any of these words that are misspelled.

air conditioner

air show

air-traffic controller

all ready

alright

baby sitter

back porch

backyard

ball-point pen

bar stool

bestseller

black-board

bowlgame

busline

by-product

carpool

CD ROM

chainsaw

church-goer

coffeemaker

copy editor

court martial

cover up

daylight saving time

day-long (adjective)

desk-top

dump truck

email

facelift

filmgoer

film maker

floodwaters

folksinger

follow-up

freethrow

ground rules

hair stylist

half-brother

home owner

hot line

jet-liner

jump shot

knick-knack

lightbulb

lineup

longterm

long-time

meat loaf

men's wear

miniseries

multilateral

Chapter 10: One Word, Two Words or Hyphenated? N-Z

NAME: _____
CLASS: _____
DATE: _____

Use proper copy-editing symbols to correct any of these words that are misspelled.

nametag

nation-wide

non-chalance

non-violent

one-time

paperwork

peace-keeper

pitchout

postmortem

pot hole

powerline

pre-election

pricetag

race track

rightwing

rock-n-roll

runningback

running-mate

schoolbus

school teacher

self esteem

semi-finals

sewerline

shut-down

shutout

snow man

spacewalk

sportswriter

squeeze play

stepping-stone

step sister

sweatshirt

take-over

teenager

tell-tale

tidal wave

toy maker

T shirt

tuneup

underway (not nautical)

video game

wind-chill index

woodstove

Chapter 11: Writing as a Journalist: Objectivity

NAME: _____

CLASS: _____

DATE: _____

A. Label each of the following *O* if they are objective as defined in journalism, *N* if they are not.

1. _____ The pope is infallible.

2. _____ God doesn't exist.

3. _____ Abortion is murder.

4. _____ Businesses don't care about workers.

5. _____ The Republican Party believes in limited government, the Democratic Party in big spending.

6. _____ Adolf Hitler was a madman.

7. _____ The suspect is guilty.

8. _____ I think the suspect is guilty.

9. _____ He looks guilty.

10. _____ The prosecuting attorney contended at the trial that the suspect is guilty.

11. _____ The candidate looked tired.

12. _____ She feels men are all alike, but he believes otherwise.

13. _____ It's been so dry here lately, the cows are giving powdered milk.

B. If the story below is accurate and true, what do we know about the statements that follow it? Write *T* if we know a statement to be true, *F* if we know it to be false and *?* if we cannot be sure.

Police are called to the scene of a traffic accident. They find that Sarah Lester's car has collided with a truck owned by Tin Chou. Lester tells police that she hit the truck when she swerved to miss a child who ran into the street. The driver of the truck says Lester changed lanes and hit him head-on. The police ask him whether he saw a child run into the street, and he says no. Police are unable to locate a child at the scene.

1. _____ Sarah Lester made up the story about the child running across the street.

2. _____ The police think Lester is lying.

3. _____ The truck was driven by Tin Chou.

4. _____ Chou owned the truck that was totaled.

5. _____ Everyone survived the accident.

6. _____ We don't know yet whether Lester will get a ticket.

C. Explain briefly any bias in the following sentences.

1. The bureaucrats in the school's student-aid department said alumni donations for scholarships are falling short this year.

2. The incumbent refuted his opponent's accusation that he was in the pocket of special-interest groups.

3. She denied the fact that she killed her husband.

4. The City Council still hasn't passed an anti-smoking proposal.

Chapter 12: Conciseness

NAME: _____
CLASS: _____
DATE: _____

Rewrite the following words or phrases, where possible, to say the same thing more clearly or concisely.

1. Say it in fewer words.

   a. Use single-word verbs rather than phrases:

assessed a fine	costs the sum of	give consideration to
make mention of	put emphasis on	has got to
head up	gather up	hurry up
is situated at	makes her home	

   b. Avoid *to be* verbs as helping verbs.

is representative of	will be a participant in	it is her intention

      The play was written by Shakespeare.

   c. Use single-word modifiers and connectives rather than phrases.

a great deal of	all of a sudden	off of
at this point in time	despite the fact that	as a consequence of
for the reason that	prior to	

   d. Avoid redundancies.

blazing inferno	bare essentials	consensus of opinion
fatal killing	freewill offering	general rule
personal friend	12 noon	armed gunman
blue in color	self-confessed	completely destroyed
whether or not		

2. Say it in simpler, shorter words.

   amidst

   coequal

89

cognizant

contusion

effectuate

finalize

imbibe

interface

maximize

orientate

prioritize

residence

terminate

utilize

Chapter 12: Conciseness, No. 2

NAME: _____
CLASS: _____
DATE: _____

Use proper copy-editing symbols to tighten the following sentences.

1. His use of metaphors is effective.
2. He knew he was weak in the area of grammar.
3. The field of medicine was fascinating to her.
4. The man ran down the street with his briefcase in hand.
5. It was her mind that he admired.
6. After setting a new record, she explained her future plans.
7. A grand total of $5,000 was gathered up.
8. The ball was hit by the catcher.
9. It seems that she is happy.
10. She thought the assignment was an easy one to do.
11. I think that this looks OK to me.
12. There are many who believe otherwise now.
13. It was this book that influenced me the most.
14. In order to get closer to the entire audience, the speaker stepped off of the stage.
15. In the immediate vicinity of the accident, FAA investigators were piecing parts of the fuselage back together.
16. The noon luncheon was postponed until later, the chairman said, because past experience told him the new construction would not be entirely completed.
17. The overhead roof was partially destroyed, and the fire chief said a fire could recur again.
18. The professor plans to write his entire book during the summer months before the fall semester.
19. On two different occasions, the unsolved problem resurfaced again.

20. They are the people who were victims of the Holocaust.

21. The higher court remanded the case back down to the lower court.

22. The accident occurred at 10 p.m. Wednesday night after the driver of the vehicle found his car completely surrounded by a thick fog, he later told police after he hit the tree.

Chapter 13: Sexism, Racism and Other "isms"

NAME: _____

CLASS: _____

DATE: _____

Edit or rewrite these sentences to eliminate (1) language that may be offensive to the people involved, (2) language that treats women or minorities unequally with white men or (3) language that excludes people because of sex, race, age, disability and so on.

1. The man charged with rape was defended by a lady lawyer.

2. Seven spacemen were killed in the explosion of the space shuttle Challenger.

3. A manager needs to know his people as well as his job.

4. She's a coed at the University of Michigan.

5. Mrs. John (Linda) Ferris, 62, died Oct. 10, 1999, of a heart attack.

6. A man and wife seem to find it harder these days to stay married.

7. Altobelli is a male secretary at the law firm of Prescott and Heineman.

8. Ms. Smith never married.

93

9. Thomas Sowell is an eminent black scholar and newspaper columnist.

10. The suspect was described as a Hispanic male of average build in his late teens.

11. A Vietnam veteran held his wife and two children hostage for four hours today in Gary, Ind., before releasing them and committing suicide.

12. A grandmother of three announced Monday she would run for the City Council.

13. Spend a few hours with Regina Esparza, and her sense of humor is so infectious, you soon forget she's a cripple.

14. She quit work when her child was born and became a housewife.

15. Irishmen have contributed much to this nation.

16. Emily Dickinson is well thought of as a poetess.

17. When you're at a garage sale, remember you can usually Jew the price down below what they're asking.

Chapter 13: Sexism, Racism and Other "isms" (Continued)

NAME: _____

CLASS: _____

DATE: _____

18. He's still spry at 80.

19. Don't be an Indian giver!

20. After the auto accident, he became a Holy Roller.

21. Janice? She's the woman over there with the butch hair.

22. She's a highly respected actress despite being deaf and dumb.

23. Mankind has been around for at least 100,000 years.

24. Washington doesn't seem to care about the common man and his troubles.

25. Barbara Ohmstead, an attractive blond physician, said she never felt as though she had been discriminated against because she's a woman.

26. Has the garbageman made his pickup yet?

27. Harvard's alumni contribute a great deal to the school.

28. The mayor was dressed in a gray business suit and pumps as she welcomed the trade delegation.

Chapter 14: Writing News That's Fit for Print

NAME: _____

CLASS: _____

DATE: _____

1. In our third approach to picking a lead, what did we say makes the strongest lead of all? What's the next best? What is the fallback position in case neither of those work?

2. What five words describe the basic formula for a hard-news print lead?

3. What are the two kinds of *who* in a lead, and when is each used?

4. What are the four kinds of *what* in a lead, and when is each used?

5. Put a check in front of the people who should receive an immediate-ID lead in a hard-news story in the Springfield News. Base your judgment solely on the description.

   a. _____ the first lady of the United States

   b. _____ the mayor of Springfield

   c. _____ a City Council member

   d. _____ a rape victim

   e. _____ Madonna

   f. _____ a local Navy recruiter

   g. _____ the head of the local Better Business Bureau

   h. _____ an assistant professor at Springfield University

   i. _____ the governor of the state

   j. _____ the governor of another state, not nearby and not populous

6. How would you write the day or date in describing events taking place on the following days if today is Thursday, Nov. 11, 1999?

   a. Wednesday, Nov. 10, 1999

   b. Tuesday, Oct. 4, 1999

   c. Monday, Nov. 21, 1999

   d. Friday, Nov. 12, 1999

   e. Tuesday, Jan. 25, 2000

   f. Sunday, Nov. 7, 1999

   g. earlier in the day Thursday, Nov. 11, 1999

7. Put a check in front of any of the following leads that suggest a topic instead of stating a thesis. (Ignore lack of time and place information here — they could properly come later because they wouldn't be top priorities in the following stories.)

   a. _____ The Springfield School Board will discuss education at its meeting this Friday.

   b. _____ A nationally known expert on fire safety lectured the city Fire Department on Thursday about preventing fires in public housing.

   c. _____ Springfield University researchers said Wednesday they may have isolated a gene responsible for aging.

   d. _____ The president gave his reasons Friday for cutting taxes.

   e. _____ The public is invited to sound off to the Springfield Park Commission this Monday on a proposal to prohibit liquor in the city's parks.

8. Check the story description below that sounds like the best candidate for a summary lead.

   a. _____ The City Council passes a no-smoking-in-public-places ordinance, tables a proposal for a city income tax and agrees with recommendations by the Planning and Zoning Commission to reject two zoning-change requests.

   b. _____ A poll sponsored by ABC shows the president's approval rating has dropped from 68 percent last week to 51 percent this week. A poll sponsored by CBS finds his approval dropped from 65 percent to 53 percent during the same period of time. An NBC poll shows a drop in his approval from 71 percent last week to 59 percent this week.

Chapter 14: Writing News That's Fit for Print (Continued)

NAME: _____

CLASS: _____

DATE: _____

9. Rewrite the following news items. Make sure that your leads are hard-news leads, that they present information in the best order possible, that they are short and clear but tell everything essential and that they follow wire-service style. These may require more than just one sentence or one paragraph. Assume you are writing the leads for Thursday afternoon's Springfield newspaper.

    a. On Saturday, the Springfield Garden Club will hold its regular monthly meeting, at Bill Johnson's house at 1311 Twelfth Street this time, at 12 noon to discuss seed catalogs for spring planting.

    b. Bill Knox of Springfield won $14 million in the state lottery drawing Wednesday. He bought the winning ticket at a neighborhood convenience store that morning when he stopped in for coffee on his way to work.

    c. Thursday morning, the Iraqis launched 10 Scud missiles at Israel. Israeli defense forces shot down all but two with U.S. Patriot missiles. Acting in response to the Iraqis' actions, the president ordered U.S. Navy ships to the area and called allies about reopening war with Iraq. Iraq gave no reason for the attack and, in fact, denied the attack occurred.

Chapter 14: Wire-Service Style Summary, No. 1

NAME: _____
CLASS: _____
DATE: _____

Use proper copy-editing symbols to fix any of the following to conform to wire-service style.

A. Abbreviations

1. 6 AM

    a.m. radio

    1492 AD

    35-m.m. camera

    t.v.

    L.A.

    UN observer

    Rochester, NY

    i.q. test

    C.I.A.

    N.A.T.O.

    USSR

2. 25 percent

    $.25

    twenty-five dollars

3. Thurs., Jun. 16th, 1998

    Sept. 1998

    October 9

    Xmas vacation

    July 4 parade

4. Reverend Jesse Jackson

    Pres. Bill Clinton

    Prof. Kauffman

5. National Organization for Women (NOW)

    Acme Co. Inc.

    Computer Company of America

    Senator Spence Abraham, R.-MI

6. Anchorage, Alas.

    Portland, Oregon

    Des Moines, IA

    Tex.

    Portland, ME

    Orem, Utah

101

7. New York City

Washington, D.C.

101 Maple Dr.

10th St.

U.S. Highway 23 S.

8. We're number one!

I-70

Airdale Ln. SE

Fort Smith, Ark.

Mt. St. Helens

Sault St. Marie

Brown v. Board of Education

Chapter 14: Wire-Service Style Summary, No. 1 (Continued)

NAME: _____

CLASS: _____

DATE: _____

B. Capitalization

1. Red Delicious Apple

german shepherd

french fries

basset hound

lily of the valley

Boston cream pie

styrofoam

kleenex

Kitty Litter

fiberglass

sheetrock

2. South Korea

Eastern United States

southern accent

a western (movie)

Drive two miles north.

out west

southeast Michigan

3. Pioneer and Huron High Schools

Detroit and Huron rivers

4. Psychology Department

English department

state department

the fire department

Ypsilanti police

tax committee

master's

President's cabinet

Board of Directors

Legislature

City Council

Democratic Party

communist philosophy

socialist ideas

5. "Let us praise him (God) in prayer."

The priest offered communion to the congregation.

The pope said mass.

6. black   Native American

   caucasian

7. Mayor Dennis Archer   Broadcaster Rush Limbaugh

Chapter 14: Wire-Service Style Summary, No. 1 (Continued)

NAME: _____
CLASS: _____
DATE: _____

C. Numerals

   1. six-month-old baby

      Apollo XI

      Air Force One

      −six degrees

   2. Ninth Congressional District

      9th Street

      5th Amendment

      First Lt.

   3. nine

      11

   4. 1/2

   5. Edwin Meese 3rd

Add 2 teaspoons of sugar.

5 mph

9-yard run

3-under-par

Third District Court

6th Ward

10th Precinct

1999 was a good year.

5 percent responded.

1 1/2

World War II

Chapter 14: Wire-Service Style Summary, No. 2

NAME: _____
CLASS: _____
DATE: _____

Use proper copy-editing symbols to edit the following sentences. You will need to consult your stylebook for some of the answers.

1. He said he could have made a $200-million dollar deal if he'd seen the opportunity ahead of time.

2. Representative Gary Thompson, R.-Ark., earned his master's from the University of Arkansas in 1964.

3. Eleven seniors joined the Rockbridge high school class on the 1st day, increasing the class size by six percent.

4. Drake University History Prof. Sid James said, "The philosophy of Communism seems to be crumbling. Marxist countries are choosing to become more Democratic."

5. The President was sitting in the oval office while a member of the Palestinian Liberation Organization lectured about 35 persons outside the White House.

6. Several saving and loan banks, some of them sizeable, went bankrupt last Spring.

7. The first moon landing marked a milestone in the space age.

8. KANSAS CITY, MO (AP) — A Federal judge Friday struck down a Missouri statue prohibiting the use of welfare funds for abortions.

9. Representative John Kasich, an Ohio Republican, said Tues. he would vote for the bill.

10. Mr. Russell Elders, Jr., 23, 3751 Fenderbender Rd., servived a one car crash into the median on I-70 Wednesday night around 8 p.m.

11. Temperatures Thursday were in the '30's.

12. The Springfield police department will be out in force when the cabinet member and the Pope meet August 2nd.

13. Dr. William Sung asked everyone in the Philosophy Department to pay twenty scents for each cup of coffee.

14. A 3rd Ward candidate has withdrawn from the race.

Chapter 15: Writing News for Broadcast

NAME: _____

CLASS: _____

DATE: _____

A. Answer No. 1 with sentences, No. 2 with *T* for true or *F* for false.

1. What are the six main differences between writing news for broadcast and writing for print?

2. Label each of the following statements *T* if true or *F* if false.

a. _____ Broadcast news often allows more leeway for expressing personal judgments, especially if noncontroversial.

b. _____ Broadcast news stories often begin with a general statement that would probably be edited out if run in a newspaper.

c. _____ Because broadcast stories are so short, no information should ever be repeated.

d. _____ Broadcast writers must be more aware of homonyms than print writers.

e. _____ Most experts agree that good grammar and spelling are of little importance in writing broadcast news.

f. _____ Every print news lead should include *who, what, when, where, why* and *how*.

g. _____ Print stories can use the time element *yesterday* or *tomorrow* but never *this morning, this afternoon, this evening* or *tonight*.

h. _____ *Time, day* or *date* should rarely, if ever, start a lead.

i. _____ Broadcasters are more likely than print journalists to put the attribution at the end of a sentence.

j. _____ Broadcasters generally prefer present tense even in hard-news stories.

k. _____ Broadcast sentences tend to be a bit longer than print sentences because they have to get in more information in a shorter period of time.

l. _____ A question lead should be used only when the question will be answered in the story.

m. _____ Clichés make great leads and snappers because everyone identifies with them.

n. _____ Differing advice between print and broadcast classes often has to do with differences in the nature of the media.

109

B. Rewrite the following items in broadcast style.

1. 17 cents
2. $33
3. 75 percent
4. FBI
5. Mister
6. NAACP
7. NATO
8. Interstate 66
9. 33 billion
10. 4.5 trillion
11. 1 1/2
12. score of three to one
13. 1608 W. Elm
14. the year 1996
15. Dow Jones index down three points
16. May 31

Chapter 16: Writing News for the New Media

NAME: _____

CLASS: _____

DATE: _____

1. Some people believe the new media will endanger democratic societies by allowing the public to read only the news it wants to read, thereby lessening understanding of critical public issues. Explain why you agree or disagree with this theory.

2. Unlike traditional media, the new media have virtually unlimited space because news and other information are called from computerized databases on demand. In your own words, describe how you would help consumers sort through this mass of information.

3. Compare the CNN Web site to the USA Today Web site on the same day. Describe differences in their approach to delivering the news online.

4. If you were assigned the task of creating a Web site for a newspaper, what innovative features would you use to ensure local appeal? Describe how you would make your site different from that of other area newspapers.

5. Using the criteria outlined in this chapter, analyze the Web site of your college newspaper for credibility. If your newspaper does not have such a site, choose that of another college.

6. Examine the USA Today Web site and describe how it uses the technique of layering in the presentation of news. Be specific in your analysis.

Review No. 1: Identifying Parts of Speech

NAME: _____

CLASS: _____

DATE: _____

A. In the space before each group of words, identify what part of speech the words would typically be.

1. _____ was   says   edits   reads
2. _____ gee   ouch   oops   whew
3. _____ smart   handsome   wicked   sexy
4. _____ barn   car   television magazine
5. _____ very   cautiously quite   softly
6. _____ and   but   because   or
7. _____ she   their   you   us
8. _____ by   on   under   before

B. Above the following sentences, adapted from an AP story, label each word by its part of speech: *N* for noun, *P* for pronoun, *V* for verb, *Adj.* for adjective, *Adv.* for adverb, *I* for interjection, *C* for conjunction or *Prep.* for preposition.

Remember that many words can be used as different parts of speech. Label the part of speech the word is in the sentence here. Also, if the word is normally a noun, for example, but is being used here as an adjective, label it *N/Adj.*

If you have difficulty, look up the word in the dictionary. If the word can be different parts of speech, look for an example of a sentence in the dictionary close to the one here.

1. The Postal Service is considering ending the practice of delivering mail "postage due" when the stamps on a letter or package are insufficient.

2. Instead, underpaid mail would be returned to the sender, just as is done currently with mail lacking any stamp.

3. Postal officials said the change is necessary because with all the families with two income earners or only one parent, mail carriers are often unable to find anyone home these days to pay the postage due.

113

Review No. 2: Identifying Verbals

NAME: _____

CLASS: _____

DATE: _____

In the space before each of the following sentences, identify the italicized word: *V* for verb, *P* for participle, *G* for gerund, of *I* for infinitive. Then, after the comma, label the part of speech for which the underlined word or the phrase containing it is substituting.

(Hint: A verb would be serving as a main verb. A participle would be substituting for an adjective, a gerund for a noun. An infinitive could be substituting for a noun, an adjective or an adverb, depending on the sentence.)

_____ , _____ 1. She loves *playing* the violin.

_____ , _____ 2. *Playing* the violin, she seemed a natural.

_____ , _____ 3. She was *playing* the violin.

_____ , _____ 4. It seems that everybody is *jogging* these days.

_____ , _____ 5. *To ask* too many questions is dangerous.

_____ , _____ 6. *Looking* out the window, he saw troops in the street.

_____ , _____ 7. The protesters asked the president *to step* down.

_____ , _____ 8. *Riding* her pony was how she spent most of her time.

_____ , _____ 9. You'd have to be awfully lucky *to win*.

_____ , _____ 10. The contractor asked the Planning and Zoning Commission for permission *to build* on the property.

_____ , _____ 11. Miller has been *writing* a novel for three years.

_____ , _____ 12. Debaters like *arguing*.

_____ , _____ 13. The candidates *debating* tonight are all independents.

_____ , _____ 14. The couple downstairs did nothing but *fight*. (Hint: The word *to* is implied.)

_____ , _____ 15. The minister said she felt *chosen* by God.

_____ , _____ 16. *Working* story problems in math was not his idea of a good time.

_____ , _____ 17. He asked her *to write* him often.

_____ , _____ 18. Her team *having* lost in the playoffs, she didn't watch the Stanley Cup finals.

115

_____ , _____ **19.** We have plenty of food *to eat*.

_____ , _____ **20.** The film star said her life was *acting*.

_____ , _____ **21.** She was *driving* fast.

_____ , _____ **22.** She loves *driving* fast.

_____ , _____ **23.** She loves *to drive* fast.

_____ , _____ **24.** *Driving* too fast, she lost control of the car.

_____ , _____ **25.** The driver *having gone* too fast, an accident was likely.

Review No. 3: Identifying Parts of a Sentence

NAME: _____

CLASS: _____

DATE: _____

A. Underline the complete subject of the following sentences once, the complete predicate twice. Then, circle the simple subject, and put a square around the simple predicate. If a sentence has more than one clause, label the parts of each clause.

1. The professor gave easy tests.

2. The professor was tough, but he was fair.

3. The professor and his assistant entertained and inspired students.

4. The distinguished-looking, gray-haired professor lectured entertainingly but gave difficult tests.

B. Label the various kinds of grammatical objects in the following sentences with these abbreviations:

    DO — direct object
    IO — indirect object
    O of Inf — object of infinitive
    O of Part — object of participle
    O of Prep – object of preposition
    O of Ger — object of gerund

1. She sent her husband flowers for his birthday.

2. Would you hand me those, Paul?

3. Sammy Sosa slammed the ball out of the park.

4. They thought him to be headed for jail.

5. Hurdling the fence, he outpaced the pack.

6. Reporting news is no job for the bashful.

C. Circle the predicate adjectives in the following sentences, and put squares around the predicate nominatives.

1. I'm tired, but you look good.

2. Yes, I feel fine.

3. Ben was there.

4. Joan, the guide, seems well-informed.

5. That's Joan, our tour guide.

6. It is I.

7. The package was due any day.

8. It's been proved. It's proven. It's a proven fact.

9. It's nice to see you.

10. It's been a while.

D. In the space before each of the following sentences, identify the italicized word: *A* for appositive, *N* for noun of direct address or *P* for predicate objective.

1. _____ *Hank,* would you hand me that coffee cup?

2. _____ The dog, *Fido,* is just a pup.

3. _____ The nurse, Ursula, sang the baby, Jenny, a song, *Bill.*

4. _____ His friends called him *Biff.*

5. _____ My sons, *Andrew and Taylor,* love watching cartoons.

Review No. 4: Final Exam

NAME: _____

CLASS: _____

DATE: _____

A. Multiple Choice Circle the *correct* answers.

1. She is one of those people (who, whom) (is, are) never too busy to see a student.

2. (More important, More importantly), we didn't know it was (he, him) when the doorbell rang.

3. (Call, Contact) Jean Stanley at 555-5555 for information about (hosting, holding) a party.

4. (Who's, Whose) coming? (Your, You're) guess is as good as mine.

5. One thing (lead, led) to another.

6. The issue (centers around, centers on) the vice president's image.

7. (Prior to, Before) the operation, she was in constant pain.

8. (While, Although) we disagreed at the time with what he said, we later decided he made some good points.

9. (Among, Between) the three of us, we can probably put together a proposal that will compare favorably (to, with) (their's, theirs, they'res).

10. He thought the shirt wasn't made (as, so) well as the ones he buys through the mail.

11. I don't know (if, whether, whether or not) I want to go.

12. He was (convinced, persuaded) that he should try to (convince, persuade) others to go to the seminar.

13. I believed (she, her) to be (she, her). Meanwhile, (I, me) was thought to be (him, he).

14. (We, Us) journalism students have it rough, but not (as, so) rough as (they, them).

15. It is (she, her), not (he, him), of (who, whom) we speak.

16. He had just (laid, lay, layed, lain) down when the phone (rang, rung).

17. The whole (composes, comprises, constitutes) the parts; the parts (compose, comprise, constitute) the whole; the whole is (composed of, comprised of, constituted of) the parts.

18. His vase was different (from, than) the one at the museum; compared (to, with) his, the museum's looked plain.

119

19. Would you (lend, loan) me your home computer?

20. She looked (proud, proudly) as she left.

21. Presently means (now, soon).

B. Sentence Editing Use proper copy-editing symbols to correct any grammar, usage, style, spelling or punctuation mistakes in the following sentences.

1. Pork and beans is a favorite Western dish.
2. If I was going to go, I would have dressed by now.
3. I'll try and be done in 20 minutes.
4. She is the youngest of the two sisters and is the most unique person I know.
5. The panel are Betty, Bill and Joan.
6. Jamal, as well as Henry, are going.
7. The new soft drink goes down smooth.
8. Between you and I, this looks easier than I thought.
9. We enjoyed him playing guitar.
10. She enjoys reading, to edit stories, and soccer.
11. To get ahead as a writer, the audience must be kept in mind.
12. Whom did you say was the better photographer of the three?
13. A reporter should check their copy before giving it to the city editor.
14. Only one of the three speakers today seem worth listening to.
15. I didn't think they'd be here but here comes the Wilson's!
16. This new perfume smells sweetly.
17. Neither Emilio nor Jane would do their part.
18. Give the packet to him or I.
19. I finished slower than most.
20. The tall distinguished looking woman is my aunt.
21. There's two people I'd like to see at a party together.
22. Hopefully, it will rain some more this month.

Review No. 4: Final Exam (Continued)

NAME: _____
CLASS: _____
DATE: _____

23. She loves editing, and all her spare time is devoted to studying for her favorite class.

24. He, as well as they, know the hidden message.

25. The winning driver was faster than anyone in the race.

26. The story about the old yellow dog is a sad one.

27. Going back for the fly ball, the sun got in his eyes.

28. She wants to not be disturbed.

29. Measles are seldom fatal.

30. The media is not to blame for bad news.

31. The number of photographers is small.

32. A total of 30 reporters are going.

33. None of them agree about what should be done.

34. Gordon only has one book out.

35. I wish I was rich. If I was wealthy, my problems would be solved.

C. Short Answer

1. The following questions relate to this sentence: *The girl hit the boy a ball.*

    a. *Girl* is what part of the sentence?

    b. *Boy* is what part of the sentence?

    c. *Ball* is what part of the sentence?

    d. *Hit* is what part of the sentence?

    e. The verb is in what voice?

2. List the three verbals. Tell for which parts of speech each substitutes.

3. What are the three cases of nouns and pronouns, and when do you use each?

4. List the four principal parts of the verb *to lie* (recline).

5. List the three tests for passive voice.

6. List the four helping verbs that change form in the conditional and their conditional-mood forms.

7. What's the definition of a transitive verb?

8. What's the difference between a phrase and a clause?

9. What does the term *nonrestrictive* mean?

10. What are the two tests for coordinate adjectives?

Review No. 4: Final Exam (Continued)

NAME: _____
CLASS: _____
DATE: _____

11. Write a complex sentence. Next, above each clause, label it as to which of the two main types it is.

12. What are the names of the two kinds of dependent clauses?

13. List the first-person-singular indicative form of the verb *to raise* for each of the six tenses.

present: I

past: I

future: I

present perfect: I

past perfect: I

future perfect: I

123

14. Conjugate the verb *to be* in the present and past subjunctive.

Present Subjunctive

I   we

you   you

he, she   they

Past Subjunctive

I   we

you   you

he, she   they